summer dreams

American Haibun & Haiga Volume 3

Edited by

Jim Kacian ◆ Bruce Ross ◆ Ken Jones

Red Moon Press

summer dreams
American Haibun & Haiga
Volume 3

Published by
Red Moon Press
PO Box 2461
Winchester VA
22604-1661 USA
redmoon shentel.net

ISBN 1-893959-27-9

Cover painting:
"spring moon"
Carolyn Thomas
Used by permission.

 **Foreword**

Summer Dreams

IT HAS BEEN OVER 300 YEARS since Basho wrote his famous
haiku *natsugusa ya/tsuwamono domo ga/yume no ato* which R.
H. Blyth renders as "Ah! Summer grasses! / All that remains/
of the warriors' dreams. " This was the poet's response to
visiting Hiraizumi, site of ancient battles, by then reduced
to barren fields. It also refers to a poem by Tu Fu on the fading
of glory. And it is incorporated within perhaps the most
famous haibun of all time, and one of the highest achieve-
ments of the form, *Oku no Hosomichi* (The Narrow Road to
the North). In this brief compass we can discover nearly
everything of value which haibun is capable of delivering.
Everyone knows the poem, but relatively few have read the
haibun, and even fewer encounter the poem in its original
context. But there is no doubt that the context deepens and
enriches even this, one of the finest haiku written by one of
the greatest *haijin.*

There are many fine poems included in these pages, and
it is possible that some of them will attain a degree of fame
and familiarity apart from their existence within their haibun.
But it is equally certain that the full life of these poems will
not be known outside of their "natural habitat".

Is this why poets are drawn once again to these forms?
Perhaps so. In any case, they are gathering interest once
again, in new contexts and culture, which once had been
left for dead in their country of origin.

And just as the forms grow, so, too, does our aware-ness of interest in them. In fact, poets and painters from so many different lands and languages have now picked up brush and pen that we have had to change our way of formu-lating this volume. What had begun as a strictly American enterprise (hence our series title) has enlarged into a cross-cultural quest which continues to grow with time. We have taken steps to accomodate these many new practitioners from around the world, welcoming Ken Jones of Wales to join original editors Jim Kacian (United States) and Bruce Ross (Canada). Consensus over what works culture- to-culture is hard to achieve, and even the present editors were not always unanimous in making their selections. There is, perhaps not coincidentally, a larger presence of writers from outside of the United States in this volume than ever before. It will be interesting to us to follow the development of these forms around the world over the next few years.

You will note that several authors and artists have small suites of their work presented in this volume. This practice will be continued in future volumes. It is our avowed aim to bring the best work currently extant in haibun and haiga to light, and multiple examples by the best practitioners will, we believe, provide you not only with expert examples of how to work in such forms, but also the direct and repeated pleasure of sharing them.

Here, then, are summer dreams: some idyllic, some horrific, some born of special occasion, some tumbled from the quotidian, some suitable to somnolence, some most definitely from the waking mind: all available to become part of your historical and literary context, and perhaps future. And what dreams will come of that?

The Editors

summer dreams

 **Stevan Allred**

Merida, The Yucatán, November 1973

I see them first at the train station in Merida, when I go to buy a ticket for tommorow's train to Mexico City. Three of them, men with long, rough cut hair, in primitive white smocks that're made from a long piece of cloth folded over and stitched up the sides, leaving arm holes. The hole for the head is just a slit in the cloth. Their best finery, worn to come to the city. They stand close to each other in the cobblestone courtyard outside the station. Two are barefoot, but the leader wears shoes.

> His wide feet
> Squeezed into a scuffed pair of
> Ladies' black pumps

The only possession they have is a large bundle of arrows, perhaps fifty or more. Three feet long, the arrows are fletched with the feathers of jungle birds, and are sharpened to fine points, but they bear no arrowheads. The bundle is bound with twine. Have they arrived by train? From where?

I try not to stare at them, but they're nothing like the Mayans, the people of the Yucatán. The Mayans are short people, with wide bodies. Some of the market ladies are only as tall as my elbows. These men are taller, the leader as tall as me, and they're thin. The Mayans wear bleached white cloth shirts or dresses with colorful embroidery.

These men are dressed for the Stone Age.

After I buy my ticket I walk back to my hotel, passing through the market on the way. I see them again, talking to a man who is one of the vendors. A large crowd of the locals surrounds them. I work my way in closer. A woman's voice behind me says the word *Lacandöoa*, and then I know who these three strange men are.

> Before *Chichen Itza*,
> Deep in the jungle, first people,
> *Indigineos.* Still there.

The market vendor is bargaining with them for the bundle of arrows. Something rare to sell to tourists. The leader rests his hand on the sharp tips and looks out over the crowd. His companions stand close behind him, frightened, I think, to be in the middle of so many people, standing so close to them. The market vendor talks on and on in rapid Spanish, his hands working the air in front of him, arguing for his price. The leader ignores him, waiting to hear a better offer. Among the many, he and I are the tallest, both of us a full head above the crowd.

> His dark eyes.
> Two strangers, tourists. He smiles—
> Be not afraid.

The woman behind me says *Estos son gente que se vende sus niños—These are people who sell their children.*

I turn around and look at her. She's Mayan, dark-eyed and brown-skinned, her face round and broad, the sort of face that's looked down on in Mexico City as provincial, Indian, illiterate, poor. She goes on telling her friend how savage the Lacandöoans are, how they make sacrifices to pagan gods, and eat only squash and wild game. *Tan primitivo*, she says, *They don't even have rice and beans.* *Indios*, she calls them, *Perros sucios—Dirty dogs.*

> She's so close
> The sweat in her armpits
> Smells of fear.

Barbara Bloom

Leaving Kingston

At the end of the city street where I expect to find another building, the asphalt gives way and opens up to a view of the lake. I stand there looking. Looking without taking another step. That's the way it always is for me. The water is always a surprise.

> open lake
> my thoughts pause
> empty

I pause knowing in a month I'll be leaving Kingston to live in the mountains of Arizona.

It's twilight. The water so still and silhouettes of the trees so fine that their reflection rim the shoreline. There is no wind. Just me breathing in and out to satisfy my need for immobility.

Finally I turn away from the lake to face the streets, returning to walk to the library just a block ahead. But after several steps I stop, turn and look behind, afraid the view has dissolved. Faded into my imagination like a mirage.

I'm relieved to see it is still there, only changed. The gentle grays have burst into golden pink and lilac of the fading sun.

After I leave this town, this street will do it again.

Someone else will stop here and stand still with wonder because the asphalt has ended revealing just the sky and the water.

remaining still
the lake reflects shadows
moving on

Yvonne Cabalona

Epiphany

New school year, second grade, Ms. Jue's class: I bring my favorite little Golden Book, *Lady and the Tramp*, for that morning's show and tell. After our lessons begin, we are told we can play with those items if our work is finished and returned within a specific amount of time. Our heads bend eagerly toward the assignments in front of us, the classroom quiet except for the occasional scraping of chairs back and forth against the floor—sure signs of classmates seeking rewards after the conclusion of their tasks. Scribbling faster, I pause to watch an unfamiliar little boy walk along side of the display table, look over each prize, and then reach for my book. Indignant, I rush to him, snatch the treasure from his hands and vehemently declare ownership of it. His question and expression of hurt, however, humbles my possessiveness: "But I thought you brought it to share?" Silent, I press the book back into his hands and return to my desk shame-faced.

> at the chalkboard,
> his small fingers sketching
> a dog's ears

The Navy Hymn

Lunch hour—every day I timed it so I would be home to watch the public broadcasting station's telecast of

"California's Gold. " Half hour gems that explored points of interest in the state's history, today's episode wasn't any less fascinating but touched a little closer to home. The location selected for this venture was the now closed Mare Island Naval Shipyard, one of the places out of my father's military past. As the commentator took his viewers on a tour of the island and spoke about its past, I was suddenly reminded of our move in November 1965—we had been transferred across the continent—California to Connecticut. A sign boasting, "Groton, Connecticut—Submarine Capital of the World", stood at the entry to the base. It was the first time we officially lived together as a family, my father's new sub assignment rotations allowing him home more than what we had become accustomed. As the cameraman stepped inside and scanned the installation's small chapel, I recalled the church our family attended. The non-denominational structure had been built to serve a community of dependent housing complexes—residences where military orders constantly flowed families in and out. At the program's conclusion, the song startled me, it's haunting melody drawing me back sharply to that time and place, to the wall-sized glass panels that faced its congregation in the direction of the sea, towards perils acknowledged but unspoken by us all.

late autumn—
ending Sunday services
the Navy Hymn

David Cobb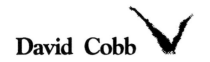

Christmas

1—the school nativity play

Six thirty. December evening. Raw weather that whisps in from the playground, following parents through the double doors of the primary school hall.

> a child blows
> into a balloon—
> the balloon blows back

Grown- ups slacken scarves, reduce themselves onto three- foot- six size chairs, suppress seasonal coughs and sneezes as the head teacher haw- hums for attention. Some announcements. Draws a monitory finger out of his trouser pocket to point to a bucket. Hopes no child will feel sick again like last year, but . . . Please look out also for the Class 6 children posted by the door when leaving. They'll be holding out basins. The collection this year is for those with Alzheimer's.

> trapped on a girder
> above the Exit sign
> a shuttlecock

Some parents pointing out their favourite bits in the handmade programme. "Isn't that a lovely drawing my Dot's done of Santa Claus?" Like a figure made with matchsticks stuck into a potato. Class One will be first on stage.

tiniest girl in school
holds
up

the star

Mrs Cavendish lifts the piano lid, removes a toffee paper stuck to middle C and begins to play "The First Nowell. " A small child with a fringe and rouged cheeks climbs onto the makeshift stage and says we're in the fields near Beffliam. The fields creak as the flock plods in, one of the shepherds sneezes over a sheep, one of the sheep waves to his mum.

nativity play—
red face of the angel
coming on too soon

Later, things are made better for the tearful angel. When Mary gets into difficulties extracting the baby from the folds of her dress, the angel helps the ox to deliver the immaculate birth.

Joseph takes the Jesus doll from Mary's lap and plonks it in a cardboard box, but one of the Wise Men thinks it may suffocate in the straw and uncovers its face. Cue for Mrs Ogilvy to prompt another of the Wise Men, whispering, "Go on, say something to the baby! "

The Wise Man peers intently at the Jesus. "You've got your father's eyes, " he says.

Joseph, shepherds, angels, Wise Men, the ass, the ox, the sheep, assemble under the spell of Mrs Cavendish's baton and sing "Away in a manger. " Mary turns her toes in

and keeps her thoughts to herself.
    And outside again.

> blurred walls—
> glimpses through the mist
> of fairy lights

2—family carols

We feel our way along the dark path to the village church, each step unsure of its landing, eyes fixed on the belfry, where shadows of ringers flicker against light cast to all compass points by a naked bulb. The peal has two bells missing, the change is never complete, but tonight of all nights this is not a blemish.

> the churchyard sloshy—
> suddenly underfoot
> a solid grave

    Mother, past eighty, has my arm around her waist. Hoisted, so her feet barely scrape the ground, I notice her weight is so little now; I feel I shall never hold her again like this; I am carrying almost a ghost.
    She is borne to where we are as close to the crib as we can get, leans on me in the pew, gazes milkily at the Christmas tree, gaudily bedecked with baubles, tinsel, but as yet unlit.
    The focus of our good nature is the vicar, an 'ancient and modern' sort of man. Warning us now, when we start to set light to the candles, not to ignite each other's coattails as well. Has provided a pail of water by the pulpit, just in case. The verger has a towel, but hopes there'll be no one this year for an early bath. Chuckles at his annual joke.

Image :: **Susan Frame**
Haiku :: **Jeanne Emrich**

autumn garden...
the wind cleans scissors
now just black cups

Susan Frame :: Image
Jeanne Emrich :: Haiku

Image :: **Susan Frame**
Haiku :: **Jeanne Emrich**

Susan Frame :: Image
Jeanne Emrich :: Haiku

Image :: **Susan Frame**
Haiku :: **Jeanne Emrich**

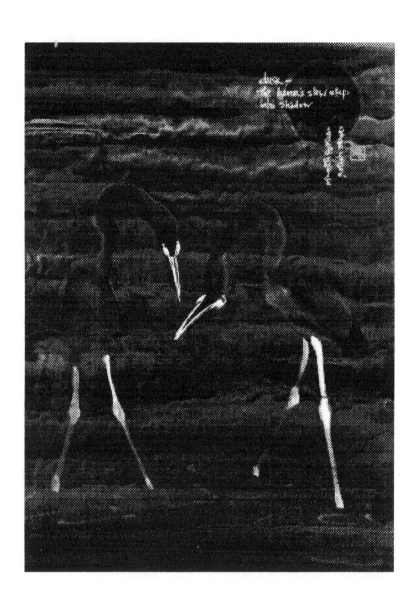

Susan Frame :: Image
Jeanne Emrich :: Haiku

My mother's face expressionless, until the organ pipes croon out hoarsely the first familiar tune. It's "While shepherds watched" . . .

> a song she knows well—
> on the back of my hand
> a warm drop of wax

Now she has a halo of animation around her lapsed cheeks, she has transformed into a Victorian schoolgirl singing for farthings on a doorstep. They have chosen her favourite, just in time. When we sit down again, she snoozes against my shoulder without snoring.

> soft touch of leather
> the woman with Alzheimer's
> worn-out purse

As we leave through the porch she slips a small coin into the vicar's hand and wishes him "Happy Easter! "

Down Epiphany Way

IN BERLIN ON A LATE SUMMER'S DAY the Epiphanienweg leads to a cemetery called Luisenfriedhof. I am coming to see you, Corporal Gabler. My second visit. After fifty years.

Monuments face each other across the gravel path, so that the acute morning sun, creating a pattern of serried shadows, strikes the blank rears of those on my left, while lighting up the inscribed faces of those on my right.

The place is full of flowers and German widows. The widows stare at me, they tend graves, some of them recording loved ones born in the very year you died in. Almost- old- comrade in the enemy's army, on the last day of the war you had a Russian bullet in the head, in the street outside your home, wearing your civvies. And me now, obligated to bring you the news of your widow, she too lying at peace, though in a corner of some English field.

Weren't we all three confirmed Romantics? The triangle has to be closed.

The sun is very warm today and, traversing row after row of tombstones, I can't find you anywhere. As I speak to you, *Wo steckst du denn?*, I wonder if it's in order to call you *du*. We were never properly introduced, we never even spoke. Just I stood beside her at the grave, holding a trowel that had lost its shape, while she laid flowers on you. That day, also in summer.

Rest, we all wished you rest, thinking of peace for ever. *Ewige Ruh'*. But now, fifty years on, when I ask the gardener with a watering can in his hand where you might be concealed, he shakes his head, tells me ñ and I know he means help—to ask at the office. A plot for Gabler? Maybe his tenure . . . ?

'Rest in Peace'—
and just nearby a plaque,
'Lease expired.'

I cannot face the office, go to the Lietzenseepark instead, where "the public are requested to respect the local residents' need of quietness." A Turkish family are spreading out a picnic, a Chinese woman goes through the unhurried postures of Tai- Chi, weeping willows touch the surface of the lake. It is still beautiful, do you remember the tulips, *Liebchen*? I think of sitting down in Babylon and weeping, and in that moment a faint shower begins.

> a sound I can't hear
> the consciousness of leaves
> receiving rain . . .

Elehna de Sousa

Hula Piko

It is here, on Molokai, that the goddess Laka gave birth to the hula. I have come to attend *Ka Hula Piko*, the annual celebration commemorating this great event.

Puna, my hula teacher, flies in to meet me and says that I must dance at *Hula Piko*. I protest, tell her that my calves are so painful from the hike yesterday that I can barely walk, let alone dance. She insists that hula protocol must be followed, which means that as the eldest daughter of a renowned *hula kumu* (teacher), she cannot be present without offering a contribution. And I, as her first student, and the only one there, must dance.

I am reluctant, but we set off in the middle of the night, driving as far as we can up a dirt trail, and then walking further up to where the ceremony is to be held. It is beneath this hill, *Pu'u Nana*, that the remains of Laka were once secretly hidden. It is pitch black, difficult to see anything but the next step in front of me. I am freezing cold, despite my long underwear brought all the way from Canada, and many layers of clothing—hard to believe this is Hawaii. We sit with the other *halaus*, blankets around us, huddled in silence, as the dancers go up in turn, invisible. The atmosphere is trancelike, the rhythm of the *kumus* drum and the chants are mesmerizing. This is *kahiko* (ancient hula) in it's most sacred and powerful form—no lights, cameras or recordings allowed—I can see very little in the dark and feel

somewhat disoriented I dread my turn, but *puna* tells me not
to worry. she assures me that like everyone else, I too will
be invisible, cloaked in the blackness of night.

> on the mountain top
> first ray of light
> —silhouette of a hula dancer

Mother Love

From the back window I see a mother racoon, baby in her
mouth, ambling across the yard and up the side of the house.
I wonder why she's out and about during the day—perhaps
something has disturbed her. She goes back for the others
and carries them one by one, four altogether—takes them
up to the roof somewhere out of sight. Then suddenly, a
sickening thud. One of the babies has fallen and landed flat
on it's rump. It cries out plaintively, unable to move.

> heartache
> the sound of it's bleating
> over and over again

My neighbour and I put it in a small box and drive as fast as
we can to the downtown Humane Society, hoping they will
be able to save it. But all at once, without warning, it goes
into seizure, convulsing and squeaking uncontrollably. The
attendant wisks the box away in a hurry, mutters something
about there being no hope.

> all day and night pacing
> the length of my front walk
> a mother in distress

Connie Donleycott

Boxes

Once again, I try to sort through the stack of boxes. Twenty- one years ago our daughter was born. Three years later, our son. I'm a saver. Baby clothes, first shoes, snips of hair from first haircuts, first lost tooth—yes, I saved those!

> tracks in summer sand
> I follow my son's
> flat feet

Small scraps of paper, drawings, schoolbooks, reports, tests and awards. Keepsakes, from birth through high school graduation. Boxes filled, what to let go?

> first day on her own
> our oldest child
> snowed in

Stored memories, saving the moments for them. Now realizing, they face forward.

> again
> a child's wonder
> in my haiku eyes

 **Robert Gibson**

Whale

Early on a June morning we are drift fishing for red snapper
a mile out from the village of Westport, Washington. The
sea is flat; the fog is thick. The boat is drifting abeam to the
current in ninety feet of water. It is very quiet.

> peaceful morning
> on the bottom of the boat
> a fish flops

Suddenly, out of the fog, two California gray whales, one
behind the other, are closing fast. The lead whale is less than
twenty yards away. I tighten my grip on the railing, stare at
the oncoming whale, and wait. Then, with a great splash,
the lead whale throws his flukes high into the fog and dives
straight down. His massive body is two feet from our faces
and cold sea water pours down on us.

And then, both whales are gone. We breathe again.
The boat rocks a bit. Water flows out the scuppers.

> ocean fog
> something huge and gentle
> almost touching

Merry Gordon

San Xavier del Bac

It isn't a beautiful structure, Father Kino's "White Dove of the Desert", and this both surprises and perplexes me. For all its baroque ornamentation it should be, and yet this is not the word I would choose for it. On the road map, it is a brown cross on an otherwise white plot of barren land. From the highway, a white speck on an otherwise brown horizon. Even as I stand before it, a beat-up Chevy blaring mariachi tears across the desert floor, blanketing the white facade of the 18th century church in a brown flurry of dust. We stand almost under the arch of the mission's massive wooden doors now, passing in between two worlds—inside, the dusky glow of prayer candles; outside, sun and stone and sky. A white cloud drifts past the unfinished white bell tower above us and I wonder if there is a word in Spanish for it, this subtle contrast of white on white.

> watching the sky
> deepen into blue around
> that white cloud

There is something vital and vibrant in this place, a quaint mixture of the celestial and the mundanely terrestrial. The honeysweet, lingering scent of O'odham fry bread over-powers the incense of liturgy and ritual in the aisles. Oblivious to tourists, the faithful pray at the gilded *retablo mayor* to cross- eyed madonnas who implore heaven on their behalf with upturned, centuries- old hands, fingers without fingertips that end in grey plaster stubs. Here and there a cactus wren pecks indifferently at the foot of a saint. We continue through the sanctuary. I run my fingers slowly along the mission's ever- peeling plaster coat, relentlessly determined year after year to strip itself down to its very core, down to the very land it was built upon. San Xavier is full of these little ironies and cosmic jokes.

"What did you think?" my husband asks me as we leave. I shrug.

But as we drive off the reservation, I cannot help looking over my shoulder.

mission towers—
a pile of sun-bleached bones
in the arroyo

Ken Jones

The Spirit Level

> In this life
> we walk on the roof of hell
> and view the flowers
> *Kobayashi Issa*

"Next Wednesday—we'll phone the results to you between 4 and 5. Do you understand?"

After the biopsy, sweet coffee in a styroform cup. Driving home the familiar sunny hills are restless now with my unease. Five days to go. Five days to finish the summer house. Wednesday dawns fine.

> Coiling and drifting
> smoke
> from a new-lit fire
> sunbright blue

Just enough worn old bricks to build the steps. I watch myself loading the barrow with slow deliberation. Cement, buckets, the clatter of this and that. And the long bright spirit level. The mortar mix—not too stiff, not too sloppy. This trowelling of mortar is balm to the spirit. I lay the level across the finished slabs. The spirit bubble sits dead centre, between its two hair lines. How could it be otherwise? it says.

She has set out our lunch with care. Two polished glasses filled with sunlight; two white napkins rather unnerving.

3 o'clock. I potter at my desk. Outside, she listens to a neighbour who has been touched by Jesus. The dark green phone waits, silent in its cradle and unbelievable when it rings.

> So sorry. It's cancer—
> I go wring out the washing
> hang it out to dry

Back to the summer house, trying not to disturb the new steps. Lock the door. Listen to the wind.

From west to east we flee together. To where the sun rises up from the sea instead of sinking into it. To where the world shrinks to a thin line between sky and fen. At Southwold, pints of Adnam's "Broadside" bitter. A jar of white honey from the Walberswick hives. Matins at Ely; evensong at Norwich.

> Blackened niche
> last year's nest
> where a saint once stood

Home for more tests. The radiology unit has an air of carnival. What shall we play for you?

> Bone scan
> the length
> of a Brandenburg Concerto

Judgement Day, at 11.30am. Yama, the bug-eyed Lord of Death, turns out to be a breezy fellow, an old school tie bright against his white coat. Obsequies seriously postponed. They can "help me live" at least until the end of the decade. I could even end up dying of something better.

We celebrate at the Owl & Pussycat Tea-room. Sipping Earl Grey, I number the hairs of my head.

Returning home, we find visitors—

> Into the sadness
> a pair of mating ducks
> alighting on our pond

Dedicated to fellow haijin John Crook, who died of cancer 16 April 2001.

temple bell ringing
one thousand times—
winter rain

Image & Haiku :: **Stanford Forrester**

intermittent rain

mahjong tiles

bumping together

W. F. Owen :: Image & Haiku

winter sun
casts my shadow - the turtle
raises its head

Image & Haiku :: **Merrill Ann Gonzales**

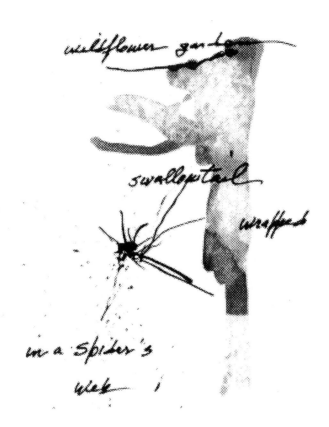

wildflower garden

swallowtail wrapped

in a spider's web

Wilfred Croteau :: Image
Raffael de Gruttola :: Haiku

crackle

of wet stones then
water chain
drips
and
drips

Image :: **Wilfred Croteau**
Haiku :: **Raffael de Gruttola**

born to the flower's insides ragged butterfly and me

Marlene Mountain :: Image & Haiku

 **Jim Kacian**

Eastertide

On a recent late Saturday afternoon, after a day in boats on the sea, we went to church. While my friend offered his confession I strolled the periphery of the old building. The alcoves where the Stations of the Cross, the synoptic 14 stage story of Christ's accusation, trial and crucifixion, had once been placed now stood empty. The gloomy light of the votive candles, the rarified slant of late winter sun through stained glass, the muted ambience of high vaulted ceilings conspired to make this absence palpable: I (long an apostate) felt oddly chastened—the more so for the purple raiment of the altar linen, the smells of beeswax and frankincense and worn wood—and was transported to the chiaroscura of my childhood, who had just revelled in the broad horizons and sharp salt smells, the clear sky and endless depths of sea that have become the arenas of my prodigal life.

> just a fluke
> returning to the deep . . .
> do I believe in God?

Heather Kirk

Boxing Day

The lead up to Christmas has been wet and cold; lingering, like the illness that has confined me indoors with the tensions of a fading relationship. Now a milder, though overcast, day invites escape.

At first the senses, like the morning, seem veiled, walking difficult. But in a surprisingly short time I feel impelled to a new, easier stride.

Inhaling more deeply, I savour the aloneness. From somewhere, a solitary bird's voice. Around me, signs of continuity—familiar lichens on stone, glossy ivy, a bay hedge wet with dew.

There are still blossoms in evidence: some, legacies of summer—a limp marigold in a border, clumps of vetch, the single rose clinging to its dark branch. . .

But now, hints of others—bulbs tipping the earth here and there, buds on a quince bush and, suddenly, breaking out from a crumbling wall, a splash of spiky forsythia

> beyond the smokedrift
> i mistook for mist
> sparks upon the path

Year of the Dragon

Staying in London early in 2000 I have a dream that one of the entrances to Regent's Park has become a Chinese gate. Over it, a carved dragon and the words 'Gateway to the New Year'.

Despite poor health, I decide to follow the dream. In February I take a taxi to Park Gate East. Walking past a small tree cascading budding catkins I see ahead two aligned fountains, icicles hanging from their bowls. This recalls an earlier dream

> last push to the top
> the overarching fountains
> still as far

At home on the Isle of Wight, one night in June I dream I'm in Chinatown and in the air before me are the solid and broken lines of I Ching trigrams. Beside them are the words of a simple dedication with a space left for the name of the speaker. Waking, I wonder if I would know when the right time came to make such a dedication.

Some days later, alone and unable to sleep, I become aware of a wish to look out of the window. And this is the moment.

> shadowy garden
> an unvisited birdbath
> receiving the moon

Later in Summer while visiting Chinatown to purchase the herbs which are my preferred form of treatment, I notice a small but expensive cake decorated with Chinese writing.

The shop assistant tells me it's a mooncake, containing only the finest ingredients and that at the Autumn Festival these are given as gifts. Wondering for whom, I buy one, take it home and put it in the freezer.

It is not until October, on another visit to London, that I think to ask a waiter when the Moon Festival is, and am told it passed a full week ago.

At home, rather shamefaced, I take out the cake and place it on a table where I keep a small carving of a dragon. Lighting a candle I instinctively apologise to the 'ancestors' for the belated offering. Sitting quietly, I become aware of the play of light

> a flame reflected
> on the carved dragon's heart
> Moon Festival

By January it is clear my health is much improved, but at the cost of a relationship that has been fraught with conflicts. I'm still collecting the herbs, though the dosage is gradually being reduced . . .

> our final parting
> a littered street in Chinatown
> at New Year's end
> clear moon, a single star

George Marsh

Man into Air

> rolling tobacco his incense
> the clang of the gate
> his bell

Here is a man—as light as a sparrow. The skin round his mouth is hard as a beak. I balance the nipple of the nylon drinking cup between his lips feeling his arm like an anglepoise against my side. His gasping widens the splay of my fingers on his ribs. He won't bother with today's local election results floating on the radiowaves like ghosts through the prison walls and he won't ever again taste a drink or confront with his withering intelligence an obstinately literal Prison Officer. He concentrates on something inward—nothing as capricious as thought, but a landscape, perhaps, an arid boundless place where the pain helps focus his attention fiercely on the hard work of trying to fly to the distance beat by beat. This is the Winchester Prison Hospital Wing, a rattling dungeon of Bedlam shrieks, dog-ends and sputum-tissue, neglected by a cheery Trusty, and a smarmy nurse. I go to find the SMO. I say that he's nominated me next-of-kin, can she tell me the prognosis—and realise with astonishment that she hates everybody, even me. She refuses him morphine, sneers, "He's devious, he's not dying"—(she has not met him yet, let alone examined him, but in the world of her projections a man of any moral stature does not, could not exist). I stagger out of her office, the words she spat ringing in my ears. "I'll give him painkillers when I'm good and ready. " Fergy deals with it better than I do. He's had four decades to learn. I am deeply ashamed that I cannot care for him, that I have to leave him there.

policing wrappers
in the spring breeze
the stationmaster pigeon

At the platform kiosk I puzzle over what a man is: *How to be a Sex God* is the cover story, followed by *Shooting Machine-Guns with the Rednecks!* and *The Berk Who Lost Two Million!* The cool names are *Brett Easton Ellis* and *Irvine Welsh*, and the photo feature is *Autoerotica*, (pin ups of cars, I think). I walk from the station past suburban gardens. A paterfamilias is mowing the lawn.

the hairy bee
sprawled on a hibiscus carpel
snoring

His father was a man—a hard- drinking wife- beating friend-brawler, who thrashed Fergy with a belt- buckle when he refused to eat stew simmered of his pet rabbit, spoon-stabbed at his soft mouth. But you can't refuse your father; his alcohol and violence rushed up Fergy's capillaries, entryists, pickling his heart, and erupted on Christmas Day as the drunken boy of twenty- one killed his girl bride.

on a path in the park
a young woman practises
quick white stick taps

Fergy has never had a sniff of a BMW; he scorns the men whose cells are ripe with girly pix, men "in thrall to bimboism," (that's his phrasing, and he calls it "self-inflicted bondage, the injustice which they have imposed upon themselves," in his gravelly mining- town Geordie). Money does not cascade through his hands in jackpot imagery: he earns four pounds sixty two pence each week. But he is a stone in the shoe of a Governor, indomitable with murderous convicts, and bracing to my bland goodwill. Over forty years of incarceration he has found the irreducible core of a man: mind, and will. There is no likeminded thinker to appreciate this. He tells me, "No- one will ever know I lived." His speech is cast in Victorian prose from the prison library, poured through the pursed vowels and rotten lungs of County Durham, an eloquence finely wrought and strange: "I am a caricature devoid of humour."

> bathers on the beach—
> the swifts will arrive
> in the next few days

Fergy is in Heaven. He is not conscious that for his last hours he has been released from his Life Sentence into a hospice and lies in a bed of lovely linen in a brightly painted room, flowered and sunned through rose curtains, and he is touched with motherly care, perhaps for the first time, by a great exponent of the Hippocratic oath whose kindness opens the sluice on my heart's pity as none of the callous neglect ever did. It is goodness that makes us cry, not suffering. Fergy is Christian and I murmur in his ear about angels and light. His body now is stiff as saltcod, drying into the warm air.

Thank the doctor, get in the car, out the driveway—that pathetic bundle of clothes! ("What shall we do with them?") —turn, where?—a sign for the New Forest. Fog is coming in off the sea and cars from the West have their lights on. Drive into the open heathland, wander out into flowering heather and scrub, chest heaving, feel for a roll-up.

> tobacco dust—
> but the cloud of mist comes
> smelling of the upper air

 **Giselle Maya**

A Bulb Discarded

One of my neighbors is a striking woman who works in a dress shop. At times her hair is blond, at others raven black. She is well-spoken, polite and impeccably groomed.

Her son is always home. Now and then he blasts rap music into the quiet village. In front of her entrance door, my neighbor keeps silk geraniums and wisteria. She takes them indoors when rain is announced. Now and then real flowers blossom and wilt within a short span of time.

I found a large chafed bulb tossed into the public flower box, discarded when it had stopped blooming. 1 took it home and planted it in dark potting soil, watering it and waiting.

Tiny leaves sprouted in autumn. One day I saw tiny furled buds appear. On the window sill in partial sun they grew. A salmon-hued bud unfolded into the first flower on New Year's day.

I wanted to show the plant to my neighbor, but hesitated. Would she care? In the end I felt that here was someone to look at and greet politely from a distance and for the moment I had no wish to get to know her better.

> winter morning
> in the late rising sun
> a cyclamen unfolds

Michael McClintock

Afternoon Garden

For the time being, well past noon, God, I ask that you above all leave me alone, that I might just sit here in the leaf shade, beside this wall with its swallow- thrown shadows and the easy, unmended thoughts time affords me: these solid forms of pots, flush with zinnias, and the sun patch fading where the grass snake glides unknotted.

> a hollow tree
> the beginning
> of dusk

Gangaa-mahaa-nadii

An old woman whose breasts are so long with age they touch the water hyacinths that float at her belly repeats a mantra that was old in the time of Babylon and Thebes.

The rim of the sun is pushing up through haze. With some hurry a few of the others who are here at this early hour remove their outer clothes and place them folded on the stone steps of the ghat beside the mother of rivers.

I do not know what their words say, but I listen and hear how the words flow through and through the street sounds: the coughing engines, the opening and closing of windows and doors, a speeding motorbike. The words become a limpid texture, holding a thousand percussions. And so the city in all its forms of cupola, tower, and walls askew, awakens from one dream to float on another, made of words.

The air is smoky from the cremations that never end; the smell is a mixture of sandalwood and cut flowers, diesel and shit.

> morning bathers . . .
> slow hands that ladle light
> shining from the Ganges

Raspados

The hour when the horned dog sleeps, that hour, and the moon a smear over the freeway, the electric plant, the brewery, the blocks of warehouses, suspended pale and humid, that moon at the end of the long avenue of trees and small homes and apartments, and the evening air a moist breath of voices, those voices at the end of all the long avenues, our voices, tired in the dark, the languid hour after dinner, tired from the world's canning, the world's stitching machines, the lathes and hot lights and liquid metals, the smell of grease and ozone, cement and tar, deaf from the buzzing saws, deaf from the hammering presses, deaf from drills endlessly drilling, ceaselessly laboring for that foot in the ass—

> muggy night . . .
> the child's moon drawing
> taped to the fridge

There is an old man from Calexico, a man mute and blind in one eye, who comes along pushing a small cart carrying rainbows of color on shaved ice, syrups of orange and yellow and green, cool fantasies in sugar for a dollar.

We listen for him, his sound a tinkling of tin bells coming out of the purple splash of day-end dreams and tree-shadow—our eyes finding him in the early evening darkness, the only man in the world good for the eyes at that hour—that man selling syrups on sparkled ice, bringing his sweet, cooling, tasty raspados.

suddenly awake—
the dog's chain
dragging in the dark

December morning
though we shiver with frost
the low sun blinds

Image & Haiku :: **Angelee Deodhar**

harvest moon
the wind-rough sea
heaving shadows

Angelee Deodhar :: Image
Christopher Herold :: Haiku

snow falling everywhere
the rumble of a jet
goes on and on

Image :: **Angelee Deodhar**
Haiku :: **Jim Kacian**

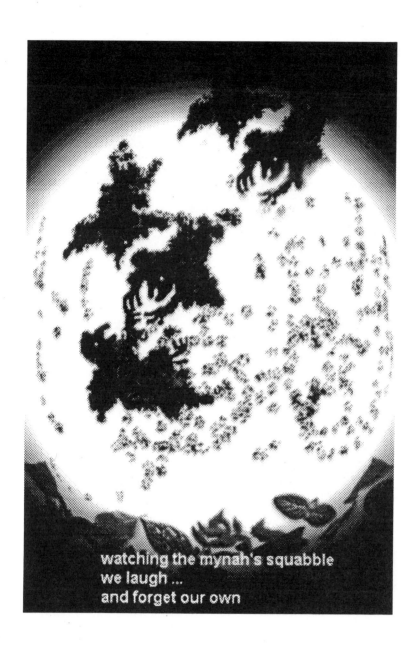

watching the mynah's squabble
we laugh ...
and forget our own

Angelee Deodhar :: Image & Haiku

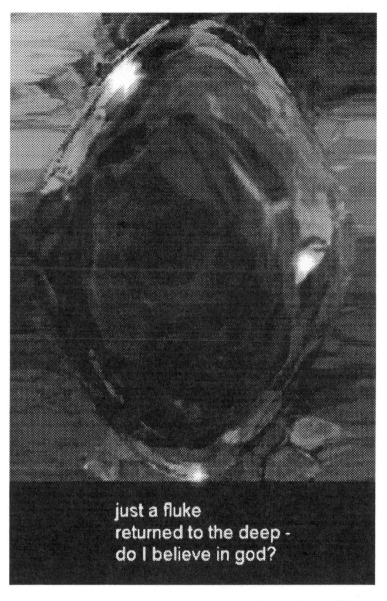

just a fluke
returned to the deep -
do I believe in god?

Image :: **Angelee Deodhar**
Haiku :: **Jim Kacian**

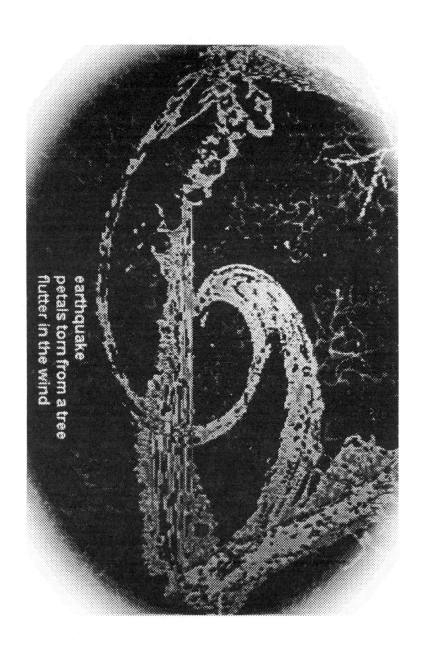

earthquake
petals torn from a tree
flutter in the wind

Angelee Deodhar :: Image & Haiku

Marlene Mountain

Hit smells right

good. You say hit cost you twelve? Law I remember when
you could get you 2 gallons for that much. Shake that up.
Looky there at that bead. Hit sure makes a good one. See
how long hit stays? Now that there used to be a sure sign hit
was made good, but I tell you a honest fact you can't tell no
more. There's a whole lot of them what puts them a bit of
Clorox in hit. Now I tell you, boys, that stuff will make you
a right smart bead too. But law that there is pretty as a
necklace.

> the moonshine:
> the beads a necklace from my throat
> to my stomach

You say you got this here on the hill above the swimming
pool? You know I won't say nothing. Fact is that's where my
daddy gets his'n. He usually goes of a evening and just gets
him a quart. Then if he thinks hit's a good run, he'll go back
of a morning and get him a gallon. He's been buying there
for years. Now I hope you ain't been getting none from
Fairview. They's mean over there. They all make theirs in
radiators and I'll tell you sis that there stuff'll kill you. Myself
I like that there Scotch.

> mixing moonlight
> and moonshine together
> and the screech of a guinea

Naia

Red Grapes

It's one of those chores that carries mixed blessings. The supermarket aisle on payday Friday becomes a tangle of carts and strollers and shoppers with children in tow. Yet it all seems worth the trouble when I stand back and peer into my pantry, arms crossed with a sense of satisfaction.

So, I grab the last item on my list, ice cream of course, and select the checkout counter with the shortest line. One must not be in a hurry here. I peruse magazine headlines as the cart and I inch nearer the black conveyor belt.

About half of the cart is emptied when two frail hands reach in and pick up the red grapes I've so carefully chosen from bunches of grapes in various stages of freshness. I like firm, crisp red grapes, and this bunch is as near perfect as I can find. After placing them on the counter the old man removes a bottle of sparkling water and, one by one, the rest of my groceries. He looks up at me and I thank him for his help. He replies, "Oh, it's nothing at all." He is slender and appears in good health despite his frail hands. I respond, "Well, sir . . . today it *is* something. Thank you again."

The shopper in front of me has a stack of coupons. It takes a long time to verify and scan each one—seasoned shoppers know this. The old man says, "I'd like to show you these photos I just picked up. I have the time, and you seem the sort who might appreciate them." He tells me that he shoots one roll of film each week, mostly of people, and things like statues and flowers. Each photograph has a story, and he tells them all to me.

Near the end of the photographs, and the stories, the cashier finishes ringing up my groceries so I break away to swipe my card and punch in the required code. Before leaving, I turn back to the old man. "I just want to thank you again for your help, sir, and for sharing your photographs with me." He smiles, as if it's nothing at all.

> chilled red grapes . . .
> kindling crackles
> in the fireplace

W. F. Owen

flares

I step inside after checking for ripe tomatoes in the garden the heat of California's summer sun radiating from my pink shoulders another Stage Three rotating black-out spins down the ceiling fan above the article I was reading that warns of increasing solar flare activity . . . supercharged magnetic particles spew from erupting sunspots at 1200 miles per second lighting *aurora borealis* for midwesterners disrupting a high-frequency radio transmitter . . . fanning my face with this page I rise to lay out the spotted tomatoes some with fissures oozing warm pink juice and seeds on the cool white tile counter . . . the ceiling fan spins, the VCR flashes 12:00.

> power outage
> a paper airplane
> floats to the floor

ring

Walking guard duty around a Quonset hut of ammunition on the Marine Corps Air Station, Oahu, my high school ring tapping the barrel of a loaded M-14 rifle. Possible racial and anti-war riots threaten the base. Tropical stars trigger memories . . . The Major in boot camp warned me that this ring would snag and pull my finger off when jumping from a helicopter in Vietnam. Instead of going to West Pac, I got stuck driving a "six-by" truck in California until boredom spurred a transfer request, which could have led to the Tet Offensive, not here to paradise . . . First week on the "Rock": this sunburn from bodysurfing, tasting *poi* (the glue-like brown paste made from taro), hearing stories on the base from Marines and on liberty in Waikiki from soldiers and sailors on R & R, about rumors of Russian tanks crossing the DMZ, moments of unspeakable terror beside hours of boredom. Alcohol-induced loose tongues, like the kid in the bar so juiced he removes the prosthetic mask covering what was left of his face from falling on a grenade. He sticks the plastic facade on someone's arm and watches them flick it off like some dead alien in a sci-fi film . . . a faint steel guitar playing Hawaiian music wafts through swaying palms just ahead of the approaching change of guard. "Halt, who goes there?"

About a year later, while SCUBA diving off the base, near an old firing range, I lost my senior ring.

> combing
> the military beach
> a crab with one claw

Jamie Parsley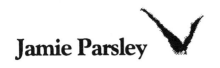

Most Holy Redeemer Cemetery, Ogema Minnesota

1.

the oldest graves lie, sagging, under 100 year old pines.
mounded, newer graves, lie along the rusting metal fence.
a life- sized crucifix—its jesus, green with moss, in excruci-
ating agony—stands at the center. a slough, filled with
migrating geese, can barely be seen through a thin haze.

> a flock of geese
> flying south
>   honk out a requiem

2.

you come here, drawn to the beauty of trees. & standing
here, you realize there will be nothing to remain of you after
you leave—no stone, no footprint in the soft earth. nothing
will tell your story. even these dead leave few traces—a
moss- filled name, an embrace of dates, sun- fading plastic
flowers. nothing more.

> an empty water bottle
>   on the gravestone—
> see! I was here!

William M. Ramsey

The Swimmer

The boy said its eyes were open. "But they're empty, like he's not at home," the boy added. He was among the group gathered, at dawn, around a pale body in the foam of the surf. Gulls hovered above in silence, then winged up the strand. It was stiff as a piling, and no one would lift it.

This is what the sea will do, coughing from chaotic depths objects that refuse to stay in it. Things carrying no message, not even a wink, spilling from the heaving surf like a fragment of some cosmic Rosetta stone.

I gazed out as if to see somewhere on the waves a hieroglyphic bird, eye, or sheaf of wheat—some ancient, coded incantation for a soul on its journey. A wind rose, the text changing into white caps. The boy galloped off making hoots.

No one's *ever* home, I thought, anywhere on earth. From the pier's railing a few tourists stared down at the frozen swimmer, and I walked off. A sand crab scuttled toward the dunes, where in a hard breeze sea oats flailed and a paper cup rolled haphazardly. Behind and before me lay the long, scalloped line of sea litter.

a sea shell
the pattern fanning
into a crack

Richard Ristow

marginal

Brochures about tombstones cover the coffee table. I pick one up and read through prices of polished and rough granite. Clever epitaphs? Extra letters increase the cost of inscription. When I put the prospectus back, I notice something . . . a copy of the King James Bible sits beneath glossy leaflets. For a moment I think about reading it. Maybe skim through Ezekiel or Revelation? No, I got my fill of angelic encounters the last time I read Daniel. As an atheist, maybe I read too much scripture? I glance around the office of Evergreen Memorial Gardens. Nobody else is here. I'd wanted some help, because I spent two hours walking between headstones and couldn't find Joe Swartz. He was an old pal I fell out of touch with. When a mutual friend told me he overdosed on Demerol, I couldn't help but feel guilty. Something always came up, and I never called when I wanted to. Still, now, at this moment, all I want to do is pour some old French merlot on his grave, say, "I'm sorry," and leave a wreath of orchids. But that mutual friend didn't know where Joe was buried.

So in the cemetery's office, I walk to the lobby desk and look for something to write with—I'd like to leave my name and number. If a Joseph Warden Swartz is buried here, I want a phone call. However, I find nothing but spreadsheets detailing cost analysis and profit margins. Looking closer on the desk I find a sales memo saying 'push burial, not

cremation. " On the walls, I see nothing but bronze plaques
imprinted with praying hands.

>Beside the wiindow
>overlooking the graveyard
>a vending machine

Carolyne Rohrig

Audition

I met her in our favorite coffee shop just across the street from the college campus where she was staying for the summer. She looked like she hadn't slept in weeks. "I don't know if I'm cut out for this kind of life," she said in a low wail so no one could hear her. "Twice now they have put me through the ringer and keep telling me to come back." "Do you want to come home?" I asked. "Noooo! I want to see this through otherwise I'll never know if I have the gift," she said with such passion in her voice that it sounded like a line from a play. "Why don't you read the letter that's in your hand?" I said. "I can't," she said. "You read it."

I smoothed it out, opened the envelope and took out the letter. "The Artistic Director and staff are pleased to inform you that you have been selected to be a member of The Theatre repertory company for the 2001-2002 season."

She sat there motionless. I read the letter again. She had no response. I shook her arm. She continued to stare. "Congratulations! This is what you've wanted for years," I said getting up from my chair. "Aren't you happy?"

> summer afternoon
> one by one
> a child pops the soap bubbles

 **Bruce Ross**

Farmer's Market

I finally got around to visiting the farmer's market in this
small town I live in one Saturday morning. The truth was
that I was just introduced to the sweet Saskatoon berry and
was hoping to find a Saskatoon pie for sale. I must have
betrayed my emotions because the pie lady questioned my
smile when she handed me what I was looking for.

I was here for the pie and for some fruits and vegetables.
I bought some beans from a woman in traditional country
dress, but there must have been something strange in my
face or bearing, for she scooped up fallen beans surrounding
the packaged ones:

> compassionate somehow
> the Mennonite woman throws in
> extra string beans

The market held other surprises than the pie. A New
Agey woman had a number of bead necklaces and other
trinkets on display but became more talkative when I told her
I knew what a sage bundle was. Also, a Head Shop owner
had all kinds of incense and oriental statues for sale. I
couldn't resist one of those statues:

> little jade Buddha
> each upstretched open palm
> with a pearl

At another table were all kinds of natural remedies packaged like the items in one of those mall chain drug outlets. The proprietor looked like a washed- out real estate cowboy and began to hustle me when I showed interest in one item:

> asthma tea packet
> "You can throw your puff away!"
> only $50

As if this weren't enough I got into a somewhat uncomfortable discussion with the people at the animal rights display table. Granted I was overwhelmed with happiness to find such a group in our town. And granted I was somewhat of a purist when it comes to compassion for animals. Nonetheless I was stopped in my tracks by what one of them wanted. With a placid smile she asked me to sign a petition for cat euthanasia. I promised to attend one of their meetings but didn't sign.

So, I returned home with the Saskatoon pie, lots of fruits and vegetables, some Austrian pastery, and the little jade Buddha. It was time to put things away:

> washing them
> the curved ridge of bumps
> on a string bean

pheasant hunting
buckshot rips
through the brush

Image & Haiku :: **Michael Ketchek**

spring moon

waterfowl rise from the pond

wing sound

Carolyn Thomas :: Image & Haiku

expanding
universe
the
smallness
of
a
pebble
in
the
zen
garden

Image & Haiku :: **Pamela A. Babusci**

murmuring leaves

loneliness

in the firefly's light

Carolyn Thomas :: Image & Haiku

gritty slice
under the pear's skin-
her voice

Image & Haiku :: **Ruth Yarrow**

in another country
from a flatcar
the milky way

Tom Clausen :: Image & Haiku

 **Pariksith Singh**

Still a Birth

Six months of pregnancy. I come back late from a sojourn. She is listless on the couch. She has been bleeding. Since when? Today afternoon. Why didn't you call me? I thought you would be home soon.

The obstetrician's voice is no less soothing. 50% of vaginal spotting during pregnancy is benign; 50% is stillborn. How much more objective can one get?

The sonogram's pulse cackles. The white flakes in fluid move randomly. Keep trying till you find it. I take the probe from his hands.

Outside, the storm has whited the earth out.

"No movement," he says.

> Snow falling
> on snow

She will be fine. Just a minor dilatation and curettage. We need to suck the remains out. Or she may get infected.

Our three-year-old is busy with her dolls. I sign the consent form and hold her in the lounge. The television set cackles suddenly.

> white faces
> watching myself
> watch the ice-capades

Laurie Stoelting

View from the Coast

Life used to be more predictable. Every few days in summer the fog moved in. Every few days someone would write a poem about the fog. Not Sandburg's fog that comes on little cat feet. A fog that pours. It free falls over the coastal hills. No twilight. Night without stars. Days spent with incandescent light.

> view to the sea—
> it's no longer clear
> what's out there

My first year in San Francisco, I read a book about the fog. About our summer coast, and how its upwelling ocean water chills the warmed Pacific air. How water vapor in cooled air condenses. This forms our fog, which is continually pulled eastward by the rising current of hot inland air. As fog slips beneath this hot air, we get an Inversion—the usual atmospheric condition is reversed. What is usual, is for air to cool as it gains altitude. But when there is an inversion, if we hike or drive up our local mountain, we' ll hit warm air somewhere between 200- 2, 000 ft. After several fogged- in days, I find myself yearning for the heat which remains above the fog ceiling.

> night fog
> climbing
> out of it

covered with stars
much of what we bring
unneeded

Hunter's moon
sharing our world view
with crickets

This season our weather is not predictable. Fog comes in
but it stays too long, or we don't have fog for days.
Sometimes a day can't decide and we hover between fog and
heat. You could blame global warming. A lot of things are
in disarray. Looking for fog, I strain to see past the western
horizon. I don't want the fog, but it's what I'm expecting.
It's like anxiety. September 11th: We didn't want the good
times to go away.

sudden heat
we enter
head first

Marc Thompson

Saturday

I don my bicycling shorts and a T- shirt after breakfast. Since
the morning is cool I wear fingered gloves. My ride today will
be 35 miles. I ride it often and know it well. About 30 miles
out there is a short steep hill just beyond an unnamed creek.
It has a sharp right turn at the top and it always slows me to
a crawl. No matter how strong I feel, no matter how hard
I try, I can never ride fast enough to break free.

> a stray cat
> picks it's way through the feedlot
> cloud-filled day

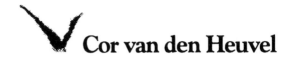

Cor van den Heuvel

Hitchhiking

It has been raining all day. I've been trying for a ride now for about two hours, walking with my backpack since my last ride dropped me off at a country crossroads six or seven miles back. Resting on the wooden post of a guard rail, I gaze into the dripping woods from under my small black umbrella. The young leaves glitter among the boles and limbs of the trees, which shine darkly in their wet-coated bark. An eighteen wheeler whirls by, clouds of spray spinning from its wheels. The wind from its passing ripples a puddle by the side of the road. As the truck disappears around a far bend in the road, the puddle is quiet again. It is in a slight depression of the sandy-dirt shoulder of the road, between the black pavement and the grass and weeds at the edge of the woods. It's just a little further on from the last post of the guard rail, on which I'm sitting. The guard rail is here because of a brook that goes under the road and through the woods. In the puddle now are only the rippling circles from the raindrops falling in a slow drizzle. One raindrop startles a bubble into existence on the puddle. It floats a little way across the surface for a moment then vanishes. I shoulder my pack and continue on, walking on the soft shoulder of the road in my sneakers. The earth gently accepts each step and then gently lets it go.

After a few more miles it grows dark. I keep walking. The intermittant traffic becomes even more scarce. There are no houses or lights on the road. I am coming to an unlit intersection.

> distant truck
> the beads of glass light up
> on the STOP sign

Snowstorm

After the long snowfall has silenced the East Village, the streetlights hold the snowy streets in a stillness of softly glowing curves and mounds of snow. Out of everyday objects the snow has created new shapes and landscapes. Garbage cans are white pillars of rounded snow. The cars parked along East Tenth Street have become sloping hills all joined together. The street itself is a still river of white, the snow now too deep for traffic. The building fronts, from steps to eaves, and their iron fences and gates have all been transformed into ornate filagrees of snow. The snow decorates the bare branches of the sidewalk trees so that ginkoes, oaks, and flowering pears are now all snow trees. There is no wind. Only a single person is out walking and now he too is still. The street glows silently in the lamplight.

> city street
> the darkness inside
> the snow-covered cars

Zinovy Vayman

A Haibun for Christina

>cheap mirror
>after the round-the-world trip
>same pepper-and-salt

I open my window. It is already dark. My childhood song sounds in me in Russian:

>*Mosk'va-Ka'looga, Los Anzhe'los
>obyedee'neelees v o'deen kol'hos*

Nine and nine syllables and a stomping rhyme. Rhyme inside the first line too. I would translate it like: "Moscow, Kaluga and Los Angeles have united in a single collective farm". Kind of stupid . . .

>in the moonlight
>star-spangled banner—
>its stripes black and white

Walking in a safe part of the City of our Lady the Queen of the Angels I still sing the short line. On Olvera Street I see a poster "Olvera Street News, Los Angeles, California. Final Edition. Printed by M. Tanzini. " I read, "Life in Los Angeles before the Americans came was an almost ideal existence. People lived to love, to be kind, tolerant and contented. Money, of which there was plenty, was just for necessities. The men owned and rode magnificent horses.

The women were flower- like in silks and lace. There were picnics into the hills and dancing at night, moonlight serenades, romance and real happiness." That's what Christine Sterling wrote about *El Pueblo De Nuestra Senora La Reina de Los Angeles* . . .

I recall my childhood full of *golod-kholod* (cold- hunger). "Cold" and "hunger' form a perfect rhyme in Russian (they differ by just one consonant). Fleeting memories of the sad charm of the Moscow countryside . . .

Russian water well:
I throw a chained bucket
into my dark face.

Haibun for Immortality

You guys are laboring hard composing, writing, creating images of yourselves and eking out your daily bread. But it is doomed to oblivion. You showed up here and now, yep. 90% of this life is just showing up, right?

A couple of years ago some people did just that. They went to work, came for the special programs and perhaps some petty business and. . . all of a sudden BOOM! and you may now find their pictures, biographies and touching details of their traces on this planet at the new Oklahoma City Museum. They are victims. VICTIMS!

If you hope to get into the similar shrine here or, let's say, in the Holy Land you are for a disappointment. Ten times more people died in car accidents on Israeli roads than in all wars and in all terrorist acts combined. You would have pretty much the same chance with Jews or Arabs though

Arabs cause four times more car crashes than Jews.

> behind Arab youths
> throwing stones at soldiers—
> rows of cameras

Once in Galilee we rode on a small bus at night. I pleaded with the driver, "Why don't you drive normally on the right side of the road?" I appealed to the passegers in Hebrew, "Dangerous, dangerous. We are in the opposite traffic lane. We are going to die. Why is he doing that?"

But people seemed not alarmed at all.

"Ah", one man answered with a smile, "If he drives on the right side not only guys behind us overtake our bus but the driver in the opposite direction who drives on his own left will collide with our bus."

I slumped in my seat.

> winter morning
> from a glass being filled
> sound of water

Linda Jeannette Ward

Dog Days

Old pines, their trunks molded into contorted shapes by years of battering by hurricanes, surround this old house now converted into a mental health clinic that serves a community where transients mingle with farmers, watermen and roadside entrepreneurs peddling everything from peaches to velveteen portraits of Jesus. From my upstairs office window I'm distracted by a bluebird hawking insects, his neat swoops flashing a colorful contrast to the glossy russet plumage of the neighbor's rooster who has wandered into our backyard again, alternately crowing and pecking at bits of cracked corn our secretary has scattered beneath the bird feeders. "Fuck you, you're supposed to help . . ." a shrill, razor-sharp voice from the therapist's office downstairs draws me to the opposite window above the slam and shudder of the front door . . .

> heat waves—
> the hitchhiker shifts her child
> to the other hip

Ulice grada.
Sunce se ponova rađa
u lokvi vode.

[city street/the sun is reborn/with the tide]

Image & Haiku :: **Borivoj Bukva**

[distance calls me/and I'll disappear/into it]

Borivoj Bukva :: Image & Haiku

[a violet/in the deep grass—/its lure . . .]

Image & Haiku :: **Borivoj Bukva**

[overnight snow/the morning wakes up/white]

Borivoj Bukva :: Image & Haiku

[glimmer of air/above the rocky earth—/summer heat]

Image & Haiku :: **Borivoj Bukva**

[water lily/in sun and stagnant water/dragonflies]

Borivoj Bukva :: Image & Haiku

Michael Dylan Welch

Hand in Hand

September 11 began with a phone call at 6:58 a. m. , California time, shaking me from sleep. It was a friend of my wife's. "Turn on the news, " she said, not even asking to speak to Hiromi. "Why? What happened?" I asked, motioning for the remote. "Turn on the news, " she repeated, and told me what was unfolding on televisions around the world. It was 9:58 in New York City, and seven minutes later, the south tower of the World Trade Center and all the thousands of people in it would disintegrate into a catastrophic heap of pulverized dust.

> the remote control
> warm in my hand—
> if only
> it could also
> change disbelief

I went to work late that day after lingering in front of the television for three hours. At work, the amount of email was eerily light, and the day passed quickly with pressured routine. Still, I checked the CNN Web site now and then for updates, sometimes other news sites, and kept seeing the same horrifying pictures.

> spreadsheet crash . . .
> as if nothing had happened,
> the receptionist tells me
> there are Krispy Kremes
> to eat in the kitchen

I was working pretty much by myself all day and didn't talk about the attack. I had a one-o'clock meeting, and no one brought up the day's events, the meeting coldly efficient in its focus on company PR and tradeshows. No one said if he or she knew anyone in New York or at the Pentagon. No one said if they felt sad, angry, helpless, or violated. I didn't say that earlier in the summer I myself had flown from Boston to San Francisco on American Airlines.

> at the end of the day,
> I clamber down a flight of stairs—
> what is it like, I wonder,
> to do this in smoke and dripping water
> one hundred times?

When I arrived home from work, my wife was lying on the couch, wrapped in a blanket, watching the news. Her office had been closed, and she had come home and spent the entire day watching television. "Not a single commercial today," she said. I kissed her and asked if she wouldn't mind driving to the beach to watch the sunset. I said I didn't want to watch more news. I wanted to find some sort of relief. A few lines from a poem by Wendell Berry came to mind: "I come into the peace of wild things who do not tax their lives with forethought of grief." She was hungry for dinner, and neither of us had eaten, but we took our jackets and walked to the garage.

                    the car shuddering
                    as the engine starts . . .
                    we both reach
                    to turn off
                    the radio

Moss Beach was about thirty minutes away, over the hill to
the west. By the time we got there, it was growing dark.
There would be no sunset because of fog, its white blanket
hugging the coast. We walked down a short path from the
parking lot to a viewpoint overlooking the waves, where, at
low tide, a large reef of tide pools is exposed to seagulls and
children. We stepped down through a few large rocks and
onto the sand, small bits of driftwood and flotsam making a
line just beyond the reach of the longest tongues of water.
     We walked a quarter mile along the darkening sand. The
tide seemed to be a little past high, and the receding water
left the deserted beach nearly devoid of footprints. A vague
glow from the west barely revealed the low layer of fog, and
we could see out across the water only a few hundred yards.
Waves sliced towards the beach, moody in their silvery,
soothing repetition. They were not particularly large, the
reef keeping them small, some waves revealing rock clusters
in the troughs in front of them just before they curled over
gracefully, smothering themselves, white in the lessening
light, white to the ear.

                    my arms around her,
                    she holds her hands
                    against my chest . . .
                    wave after wave
                    beats upon the shore

As the muted daylight grew even darker, another couple appeared at the viewpoint behind us. Hand in hand, they stepped at the same time from a large rock, landing together on the hoary sand. Hiromi said that the waves looked like ghosts, dispelling onto the shore one by one by one. We didn't stay long, as my wife felt a bit frightened by even gentle waves near dark, so we strode back to the path. We left behind a single car in the shadowy parking lot.

> sweeping headlights—
> out of sight
> hidden by fog
> the sun sets
> on the day's darkness

Back across the hill, we drove to a little burrito shop, and stood in line to order burritos. At the end of one wall, covered with a mural of a Mexican town square, a TV blared out the news in Spanish. As the line grew shorter, the news turned to the story of all the people who had jumped from the top of the World Trade Center to escape being burned. One after another after another, the TV showed clips of people jumping, arms flailing, bodies twisting and turning as they fell, so tiny against the never-ending wall of the massive building. But the wall did end, repeatedly, yet the cameras failed to capture the last moment of life in those swiftly falling bodies. One after another they fell, the terror described by the newscaster in Spanish. Without knowing what he was saying, I felt the cold rush of wind, imagined the dreadful panic of having to choose between death by fire and the exhilarating finality of leaping into the bottomless New York air. I remembered my one visit up the Sears Tower in Chicago and the amazing scale of its height above the street, above the city, above the world, and thought how deeply terrible it would be to fall from that pinnacle, the air squeezing tears from your eyes as you streaked to your death.

"*Què usted desea?*" I was asked, also being nudged by my wife. I turned from my transfixed stare at the television to look at the girl behind the counter. "Sorry," I said, and she smiled. It was such a brief and slightly tired smile, a nearly imperceptible upturn of the corners of her mouth, but it was enough to say she understood. In that moment I felt like I understood her, too, her there behind the counter, watching today's news all day while she took orders for burritos and tostadas.

> pen in hand,
> she waits for my order:
> a vegetarian burrito, please,
> with no sour cream—
> a death toll in Spanish

Driving the rest of the way home, traffic still seemed lighter than usual, the cars moving slower than they usually did, reminding me of the day the Gulf War started. I thought of the horrors of war I had heard from my parents and grandparents, in books I had read, in movies I had seen, all of it not really real, but I felt thoroughly grateful for the ocean I could listen to in peace through the sacrifice of others. I thought of the wanton disregard for human life that had brought unspeakable tragedy to the country on this appalling day. Then I thought of the couple whose picture I had not seen, but whose story I had heard, who had jumped together from the World Trade Center, falling to one death by escaping another, leaping together, hand in hand.

my wife reminds me
to keep my distance
from the car in front

her hand stays
upon my thigh

 **Jane Whittle**

Hunters

> a cackling of hens
> black flickers at my feet
> sleek bright-eyed mink

The animal flattens itself against the ground like a fur snake, motionless, watching me. I turn my head carefully, looking for a weapon, pick up a small rock.

Once, after a visit from one of these creatures, I found a precious pair of black ducks headless in their house. Mink are not a native of British rivers, but, released from captivity by Animal Rights activists, have bred so successfully they are now a deadly predator.

But this one is a baby. It is too scared to move—an easy target. One second stretches to three. That bright eye is fixed on me, the coat so sleek and glossy, so beautiful.

I cannot do it.

As I move it leaps up the wire like a dark flame, and out through larger mesh into the field. The hens are still cowering under the blackthorn. I feel sick. Will it return? It can climb anything, creep under a loose door, through any small gap like a snake. How many are there? A nest of snakes—enough for a coat—each one lethal.

The voice of my education said to me, "O He must be killed". D. H. Lawrence felt he missed his chance "with one of the lords of life" and was left with "something to expiate; a pettiness".

So I let it go, and will never forgive myself if I lose my last two ducks. I retreat, and watch. The garden is still and warm. Two lovely roses, Peace and Compassion are in flower for the second time, tomatoes redden, golden squash hang heavy on the vine—Indian Summer—the most peaceful time of the gardening year. For how long? Suddenly the ducks flee the pond in a flurry of iridescent wings and water.

> on the sunlit grass
> two black ducks change shape
> rigid with terror

I shut them up in their house and set the squirrel trap, baited with a sardine.

Later, when I shut up the chickens, a huge Hunters' Moon rises from banks of dark cloud. The trees throw long shadows across the grass and the darkness is alive with nocturnal creatures. I close the hen- house door and remove the ladder, having first looked inside to make sure they are all there—with heads.

I spend a restless night, listening. The moon is too bright.

In the morning the young mink is in the trap.

> wild young hunter
> caught behind bars
> how can I kill you?

I delegate the job.

A week later, on another perfect autumn morning, I let the ducks out onto the pond as usual, watch them chase round the island, plumage flashing purple and emerald in the sun. At lunchtime they are gone—not a sign or sound of struggle, not even a feather. I grieve for them all that day, watching the late sunlight shimmer on the empty pond, blaming myself.

The next morning—Tuesday, September 11th, 2001— another fine day. By lunchtime the world has changed.

> poised for that kill
> each minute heavier with hate
> than hunger

What is a pair of sitting ducks, here or there, now ?

> watching this night sky
> one of these September stars
> might fall—anywhere

There and Back

I haven't seen you for several months and now we are driving to the cross-channel ferry, on our way to a family wedding in Brittany. We share a rare feeling of being on holiday, together, neither of us knowing what lies ahead.
We board the Condor—a very fast and comfortable hydrafoil—to St Malo.

> crossing the water
> our double wakes
> tip over the edge

We drive on into the night, carrying a can of diesel because there is a tanker drivers' strike in France. I am hungry and want to stop in a pretty medieval town where late diners are sitting under umbrellas beside a river. You decide that waiting half an hour for a table would make us too late. We find another restaurant but they serve the meal so slowly we begin to think we may have to sleep in the car. We will blame each other for this. When we find somewhere still open the relief is enormous, more so because this journey seems to be a kind of experiment. Can we enjoy it together? After fifty years of marriage we are not sure. Finding somewhere to stay at such a late hour seems to be a good omen. I relax and begin to count every moment as a blessing. We can laugh again.

> fuel crisis
> shutting down the garages
> opening up the roads

The next day is as hot as a mediterranean summer. After the marriage in the village church a traditional Breton feast is held in a monastery garden. It is the night of the harvest moon. Trestle tables are laden with fresh sea food and champagne in buckets of ice.

> black-haired bride
> white cotton dress   hand-printed
> with a blue moon

A suckling pig is barbecued in a stone barn and served by two white-haired women. Their sons, who cooked it, carry it in on their shoulders, accompanied by bagpipes and bombards— an ancient triplet shrill enough to split the scull. We are an international company. The French talk, the Spanish sing and dance, the English eat and drink and the Norwegians watch us sticking together.

> when the dancing starts
> old legs no longer can obey
> the heart beat

This is my second Celtic journey this year, my second visit
to a painters' town. In June I travelled from Wales to St.
Ives and now we are in Port Aven, where Gauguin settled
with his friends and fell in love with Bretan fishing boats and
bonnets. The Celtic saints crossed the water in small
boats from Ireland, Wales and Cornwall to this rocky French
coast as pilgrims. My painting pilgrimage included the
religious paintings by my Cornish aunt in the little church of
St Hilary. Here, in Port Aven, Gauguin had made the
famous yellow Christ for the chapel of Tremalo in 1880, the
year my aunt was born. Now I see how her work was
influenced by his.

> painted saints, barefoot
> in the daisied grass, hands spread
> to hold the birds

I swim in the blue Atlantic, in my clothes, which dry in half
an hour. We sit in cafes with friends and relatives, enjoying
food and wine and an unexpected late summer. Then we set
off again on small roads in a direct line across the country,
from Tremalo to San Malo, following limestone ridges for
most of the journey, coast to coast. There are Celtic crosses
at intersections, Roman and pre-historic remains, and
distant horizons on either side. This must have been a
pilgrims' way too.

> we come together
> on the high road, with a clear view
> both ways

My old track- finding excitement returns, but I am no longer sniffing out ancient routes alone, on foot with a rucksack on my back. Now I sit in the car and map read while the driver seems unexpectedly happy to follow directions. We avoid motorways and towns, passing through old villages on empty roads. We stop for pastis and crèpes beside a 15th century covered market.

> plane trees at midday
> patterning the pavement
> our two faces

We find a lake, hidden by rocky hills and forests, deserted and strangely silent. On the shore small stones and tree roots are coated with bright green slime.

> we do not linger
> by the green polluted lake
> where no birds sing

Searching for somewhere to sleep that night, *Abbey de Mon Repos* sounds more hopeful. At the confluence of two rivers there is a green meadow and a scatter of ruined stone arches. It looks like a dream.

> *Son et Lumiere*
> the past shut for the season
> rows of up-turned chairs

Madam is taken aback by our arrival; Monsieur, in fringed jeans and stetson hat, is playing old songs on an electric keyboard. Bare bulbs flash on and off—pink and purple—the sky grows dark.

We order beer and sit to drink it under a big umbrella. Lightening is flickering behind the ruined arches, as big drops of water begin to fall from the sky. Thunder rolls over the old stone walls. Tall trees sway and sigh.

Beside us a young girl is playing with leaves and pebbles under an archway, decorating the steps with damp confetti collected from the gravel—another wedding. Her absorbtion is not quite real—she is listening, as we are, to the clashing of saucepans and her parents' voices raised in anger coming from the kitchen.

> *Abbey mon Repos*
> lightning flashes, thunder rolls
> disco—"Do it My Way"

The meal, when it arrives eventually, exceeds all expectations.

> *Nouvelle Cuisine*
> creations of a stormy cowboy
> petals on a plate

In the bedroom under the old clock tower Pierrots cavort across the ceiling and doves coo from their nests in the eaves. I think we are happy. We complete the journey of St. Malo together, over land and water, both ways, there and back. But, the next day, in old, familiar surroundings, what happens? Too much pain remains here. An overheard telephone call—then it is time to catch my train.

> holding hands tight
> at the edge of the gap
> opening between us

Alison Williams

Departures

The train arrives, its late. A few people talk, their voices carry in the evening chill. ". . . no, I haven't seen him, not since, oh, I don't remember when . . ." Most take their seats in silence. From the platform, she smiles and waves goodbye. Five minutes later she turns, shrugs, waves one last time, and walks away. ". . . he'd just say cheerio and go, now I could never do that . . ."

> first spots of rain
> the blue seat back
> worn pale

He does the crossword, I don't tell him, you spell tryst with a y. The wet street, two boys in the lamp light, their silent concentration, heads bent over Gameboys. ". . . but you know, its not supposed to be like that . . ."

> illegible graffiti
> scratched deep into
> the window

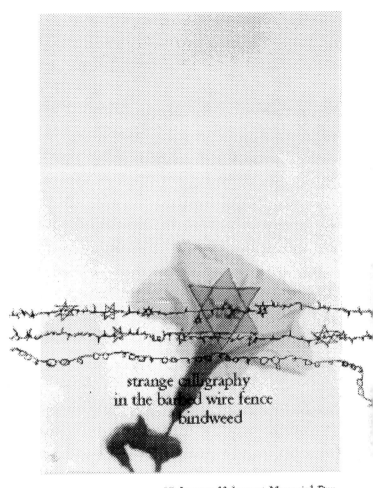

strange calligraphy
in the barbed wire fence
bindweed

27 January Holocaust Memorial Day

Image :: **Tamasudare**
Haiku :: **Paul Conneally**

the overlook trail—
    an unknown bird's song
        leading upward

Jennifer Quillen :: Image
Elizabeth Howard :: Haiku

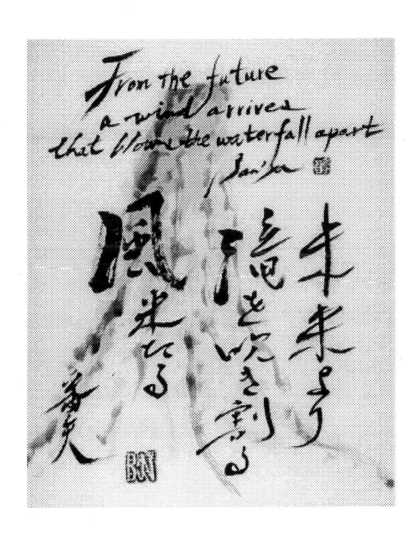

Image & Haiku :: **Ban'ya Natsuishi**

new grave —
the trampled grass
already recovering

A. C. Missias :: Image & Haiku

on a river rock
a dragonfly nymph is drying,
slowly wings unroll

Image & Haiku :: **Karen Kubara**

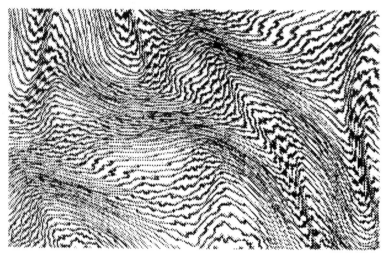

the sun-warmed sea not knowing where I leave off

Jim Kacian :: Image & Haiku

Bill Wyatt

Ancestral Voices on Kos

Arrived at appartments in the early hours of morning. A meteor flew across the balcony & gone in the blink of an eye. Sky glittering with stars, Orion my neighbour. Distant hoot of an owl—

> Waiting for the moon—
> clouds drift by like orphans
> banishing my sorrows

Up early for breakfast. Then a short walk across the main street of Tigaki, once a small fishing- village. Flamingoes winter here in small numbers. Sometimes white Storks & pelicans drop by, on their way to Northern Turkey & Eastern Europe. October, the month when the festival of Thesmophorica is celebrated. Held in honour of Demeter & only attended by women, to assure the fertility of the fields.

Back at Tigaki for the evening meal—

> Impromptu dance
> to Zorba the Greek—waiters
> spring into autumn

> October's full moon—
> from the taverna, 'doo-wop'
> mingles with cicadas

Mosquitos a problem. After an evening of wining & dining, I'm in no fit state to combat them. Defenceless, when I retire to bed, straight into the arms of sleep & Demeter. In the morning wake up to many lovebites—

> As an offering
> to this floating world—my blood
> accepts the mosquito

Just outside the hotel found several plants new to me. On looking them up, turned out to be Bladder Hibiscus. Pale, large, solitary flowers, yellow with dark purple centres, opening only in early morning. Native of Asia.

> Just like an autumn leaf that has lived its day—
> soft breeze whirls me away
> > *after Theocritus*

Theocritus, the Sicilian & bucolic poet lived on Kos for a while. He wrote one of his most ambitious poems here, the idyll knows as *The Harvest Home*, in which he describes the Koan countryside, with its singing linnets & larks, bees that loitered above fresh flowing streams. When "elms & black poplars make a shady place/ its green freshness roofed in by unkept leaves"

> Cicadas welcome
> in the evening twilight—
> ancestral voices

The Early Days of Throssel Hole Priory

Back in 1972, having become fed up with the world (or so I thought at the time), a unique opportunity arose. The previous year I had attended a sesshin at Purley, Croydon, Surrey. I had gotten wind of an English Zen Teacher, who had studied and practised Soto Zen in Japan. She had gone to America where she established a Zen training monastery. As England was her native land, the Rev. Master Jiyu Kennett came back over here in 1971, to conduct a couple of retreats. I was fortunate enough to catch the tail end of the retreat. I became so impressed with her that I undertook lay ordination, recieving the name of Zengetsu Kembo (which translated into English came across as the moon of zen shining over the cliffs). Rev. Master Jiyu returned to America, vowing to come back the following year. She was soon followed by an Englishman, whom she ordained as a monk. He came back to England as Rev. Daiji Strathern in 1972.

I met up with him and he told me that he had come into an inheritance, and was about to purchase an old farm in Northumberland, with the view of turning it into a monastery. I was working as a gardener at the time, and jumped at the chance of going up to Northumberland with him.

> Northumberland pipes
> welcome me—memories return
> with the fading light

Throssel Hole Farm (its name being taken from the throstle, or song thrush, which nested in the eaves, now an endangered species), had been taken over by a bunch of hippies and was run as a commune. When we arrived, the farm and surroundings were in a bad state of repair. We spent a couple of months doing the place up, painting and decorating the property in anticipation of the Rev. Master Jiyu's arrival. A lot of hard work went into preparing the old farmhouse. Though it was still very basic, it became liveable.

> Walking up the hill—
> but no longer a burden
> the clouds on my back

Rev. Master Jiyu arrived with monks from Shasta Abbey, California. Four sesshins were conducted during that summer, and on the first one, I undertook ordination as a junior monk. During the summer period I was given the opportunity to become Tenzo (Chief Cook), a responsibility from which I shuddered. I had never cooked before, apart from the occasional vegetable curry. The cooking was basic, as we only had an aga and limited budget for food. During this period I acquired a reputation for steamed puddings and custard! Ideal for the Northumberland climate. Another speciallity being 'toad in the hole' and scotch eggs, made from peanuts, flour and herbs. We survived.

> Remembering that
> full moon haiku—nearly
> burnt the porridge!

Throssel Hole Priory, as it was then called, became the first and still is the only Zen monastery in England. Looking back, I can only say that this was a wonderful opportunity to engage with a long line of Zen ancestors, and a rare chance to encounter the Buddha's teachings.

> A face appears
> through the zendo window—
> full moon of autumn

At the end of the summer period, I undertook the ceremony of Nyudo-no-hai, whereby I became Chief Junior, whose task it was to lead all the other trainees. As well as being Tenzo, I was now responsible for everyone else. I was also given the job of Ino, Chief Disciplinarian, and further duties were added. But I survived and learnt that I had so much more to learn. Rev. Master Jiyu returned to Shasta, leaving the Rev. Mokurai (Silent Thunder), as prior, and me as his Chief Junior for the next year. Autumn drifted in winter.

> Snoring so loudly
> not even in harmony—
> monks in the zendo

I remember snow bound weeks, frozen toilets and wash bowls. One morning, awakening everyone for morning service and zazen, only to find that our zafus were covered by a couple of inches of snow that had drifted in through the eaves. I remember paraffin stoves to keep us warm at night, camp beds to sleep on.

> Morning service—
> the snow on my zafu
> was it a dream?

Winter drifted into spring, with the arrival of the Rev. Master Jiyu and three monks from Shasta Abbey. Four retreats were held during this period, and 35 people received lay ordination, whereby they affirmed their commitment to do good, cease from evil, and help others. On the first retreat, Rev. Mokurai completed his duties as prior with the ceremony of Jodo, and I as Chief Junior, was examined in the ceremony of Hossen, "Dharma Battle", whereby I had to answer (mondo) questions put to me from the other monks. I remember a great feeling of peace descending upon me as I answered their questions, yet feeling at the end of it, that there was still so much more to learn.

> After all those years
> plunging into the void—
> no moon, no finger

The summer retreats intensified. For the most part, my duties as Tenzo would occupy me for a good part of the day, and left me out of the talks and lectures given by Rev. Master Jiyu, there were however occasions when she would let me sit in on talks given to the senior monks, and I no longer felt left out. It was very intense during this period, and I remember one of the lay people coming up to me saying that my eyes were like spinning tops and how could I keep up with the pressure?

By now, training no longer seemed like a chore, and I would not become disconcerted as the work load increased. The more difficult it seemed, the more I would respond positively. It was a time when I thrived on what would normally be described as stress. I learnt that ultimately there is nothing that could harm me, save my own delusive thinking.

> What's it all about?
> samsara and nirvana
> nothing but snowflakes

I was taken aback, when the Rev. Master Jiyu said that I was ready for transmission. Of course, I had read about it, but only vague hints, shelved in mystery. This would put me in direct line with all our ancestors, going right back to Shakyamuni Buddha. I felt that I was not ready for it, but as Rev. Master Jiyu explained, transmission only occurs when the teacher has acknowledged that the trainee has changed and wants to do something about his or herself. Transmission was not the end, but rather the true beginning of training.

> Early autumn frost—
> a woodpecker, pecking holes
> in eternity

I will be forever indebted to Rev. Master Jiyu for having that faith in me, a faith that I always lacked.

Rev. Master Jiyu invited me out to America, and I took up a years further study and practise at Shasta Abbey. But, after a while, ultimately, or my own decision, I decided to return to lay life as a gardener back in England.

> Afternoon zazen—
> late autumn snow turns to rain—
> this dream within a dream

I moved to Bexhill on the Sussex coast, working as a hospital gardener for a couple cf years. All the while remembering the advice that Rev, Master Jiyu had given me, that if nothing else, meditation would give you peace of mind, but only if you kept it up.

I attended a couple of retreats in the early 1980s at Throssel, but due to misunderstandings and karmic circumstances I was not to return again for another 18 years.

By 1996, Rev. Master Jiyu had passed away, unbeknown to me. I was not to find out until a couple of years later. Throssel Hole had now become an Abbey, with priories scattered throughout the country. The monastery has increased in size, with new buildings and 50 or so monks, both male and female.

> Morning zazen—
> rain on rooftops, in one ear
> and out the other

Having attended 2 week-long retreats in 1998, I made the decision to return as a lay person for a period of 6 months in the following year.

Out of respect, and in memory of my teacher, I offered my services to help out in the Rains Retreat of January and February 2000. I worked in the kitchen, preparing and cooking food for the monks and community. When not doing this, the time would be spent in meditation. I made lots of new friends, and no longer felt homeless, as I had for the previous few years.

> Night of endless rain—
> how refreshing the sound
> of the zazen bell

Wading through,
And wading through,
Yet green mountains still

Image :: **Kuniharu Shimizu**
Haiku :: **Santoka**

I walk -
Letting perch on my knee,
A dragonfly

Kuniharu Shimizu :: Image
Santoka :: Haiku

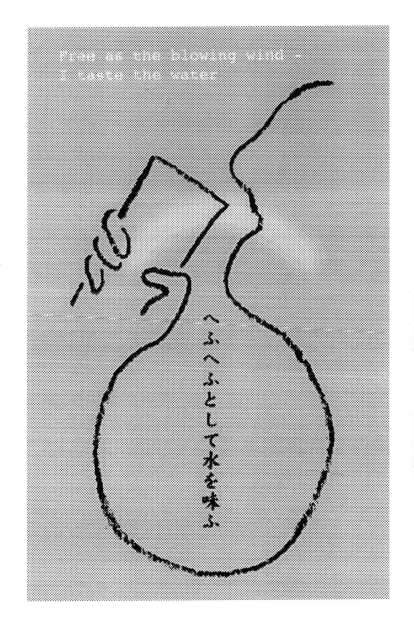

Free as the blowing wind -
I taste the water

へへふへふとして水を味ふ

Image :: **Kuniharu Shimizu**
Haiku :: **Santoka**

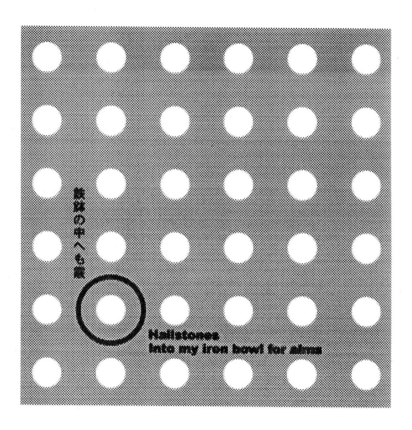

鉄鉢の中へも霰

Hailstones
into my iron bowl for alms

Kuniharu Shimizu :: Image
Santoka :: Haiku

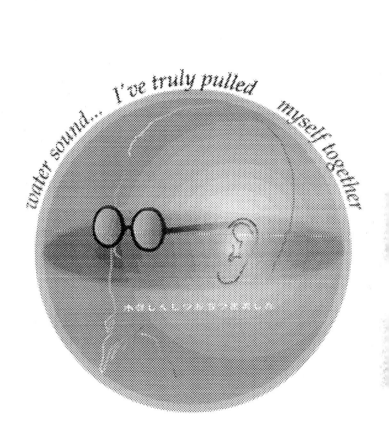

water sound... I've truly pulled myself together

Image :: **Kuniharu Shimizu**
Haiku :: **Santoka**

Let it dissolve—
my silhouette from behind
into the winter drizzle

Kuniharu Shimizu :: Image
Santoka :: Haiku

 **Contributors**

Acknowledgments

Cobb, David—"Down Epiphany Way" first appeared, in a considerably different version, in *Haiku Spirit* 20; "School Nativity Play" appeared in *Blithe Spirit* 8:4.

Ristow, Richard—"marginal" first appeared in *Bottle Rockets* 3:1.